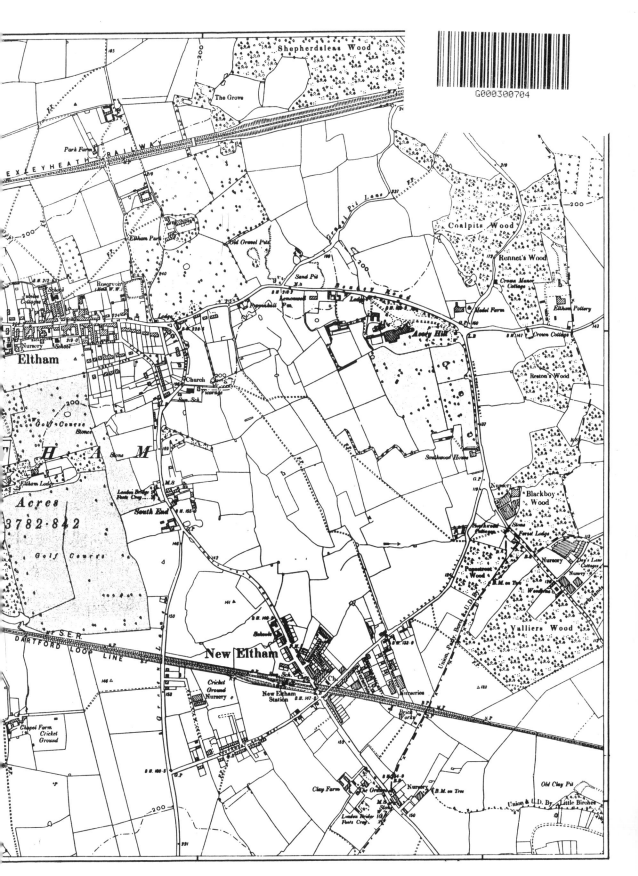

Map of Eltham, 1898

11.12.95

To
DAD
on his 65th
Birthday
love Karen, Lee & family
x x x

ELTHAM
A Pictorial History

Moat bridge at Well Hall Pleasaunce in the 1930s

ELTHAM
A Pictorial History

John Kennett

Phillimore

1995

Published by
PHILLIMORE & CO. LTD.,
Shopwyke Manor Barn, Chichester, West Sussex

ISBN 1 86077 004 5

Printed and bound in Great Britain by
BIDDLES LTD.
Guildford, Surrey

List of Illustrations

Frontispiece: The moat bridge at Well Hall Pleasaunce in the 1930s

Acknowledgements

The written research for this book has involved the use of a variety of printed source material and information that I have gathered about the history of Eltham over the past three decades. Assistance has also been received from fellow members of The Eltham Society, members of my former Eltham Past and Present adult education class, and residents of Eltham. I am particularly grateful to the staff of the Greenwich Local History Library for assistance and the use of their facilities. I would like to thank the following people for allowing me to take copies or to reproduce their pictures in this book: Mr. K. Brocklesby, 117, 134, 148; Mr. F. Coldwell, 111, 133; Mrs. J. Deacon, 119, 154; Mr. E. Dickerson, 151; Mr. A. Diggles, 124; Miss E. Edmunds, 101; Mr. D. Green, 14; Miss D. Greenway, 56; Mr. L. Hardwell, 73, 77; Imperial War Museum, 105-7; Mrs. F. Jerram, 113; *Kentish Times*, 179; Marks and Spencer, 160-1; Mr. T. McDonnell, 116; Mrs. J. Milan, 130; *News Shopper*, 178; Mr. D. Parker, 122; Mr. M. Payn, 90, 91; Fr. P. Rea, 53; Mr. R. Roffey, archivist, S.E. Co-op, 155, 164; Mr. E. White, 114; Mr. Gus White, front cover illustration, 24, 34, 41-3, 54, 57, 64-5, 68, 72, 84, 85, 86, 88, 89, 93, 100, 102-4, 127, 144-7, 149, 162-3, 165, 166, 173; Mr. B. Williams, 110. All other illustrations are from my own collection.

Introduction

Eltham and its Development

With the formation of larger London boroughs in 1965 the Metropolitan Borough of Woolwich, which included Eltham, was absorbed into the London Borough of Greenwich. Eltham's distinctive character of residential development interspersed with lungs of open space became part of a borough whose northern boundary spans the side of the river Thames between Greenwich and Abbey Wood.

Between 1832 and 1885 Eltham was represented in Parliament by the M.P. for the constituency of the Western Division of Kent. From 1885 to 1918 Eltham became part of the Woolwich constituency. Since 1918 Eltham has been in the Woolwich West parliamentary constituency but following recommendations of the Boundary Commission the name was changed to Eltham in 1983. Eltham's link with Kent since recorded time was severed in 1889 when, by an Act of Parliament, it was incorporated into the new County of London.

The boundary of Eltham can be traced back over many centuries and extends to Shooters Hill, Blackfen, Chislehurst and Lee. Within the Eltham boundary are the areas known today as Well Hall, Eltham Park, Avery Hill, New Eltham, Coldharbour, Mottingham, Horn Park, Middle Park and parts of Lee.

The subsoil of much of Eltham is clay except the Eltham High Street area which resides on a large outcrop of sand; rainwater dispersal here is not a problem as in other local areas. Surprisingly there are only a few visible streams like the river Shuttle at Avery Hill Park and the river Quaggy between Mottingham and Sutcliffe Park. Other streams have been put into closed culverts and are only discernible on old maps or drainage plans.

Eltham was once covered with large tracts of forest whose tree cover provided a home for wildlife. Oxleas Wood, on the southern slopes of Shooters Hill, has survived from ancient times. Road names like Crown Woods, Alderwood, Sidewood, Rennets Wood, Southwood and Colepits Wood are a reminder of some areas of former woodland.

1 Eltham parish boundary marker of 1894 at Mottingham Road. This stone can be seen on the grass verge between Beanshaw and William Barefoot Drive on land which was once part of Coldharbour Farm.

The presence of a Roman small-holding in Eltham has been unearthed at Archery Road. Fragments of coarse pottery, a hut floor, mortars, Samian pottery and a bronze pin were discovered. Evidence from this site is kept at the Greenwich Borough Museum at Plumstead. In addition, the museum collection includes pottery vessels from a Roman cremation which were found at Glenesk Road in 1913 when the Corbett Estate was being constructed. Coins have been unearthed at other locations including examples from the time of the Roman Emperors Hadrian and Maximianus I.

The first recorded use of the name 'Eltham' is in the Domesday Survey of 1086. The name 'Eltham' is considered to mean 'Elta's Homestead' and is probably of Anglo-Saxon origin. The Domesday entry states that:

> Hamo the Sheriff holds ELTHAM from the Bishop. It answers
> for 1½ sulungs. Land for 12 ploughs. In lordship 2 ploughs.
> 42 villagers, with 12 smallholders have 11 ploughs.
> 9 slaves; meadow, 22 acres; woodland, 50 pigs.
> Value before 1066, £16; when acquired £12; now £20
> Alfwold held it from the King.

Following the death of Hamo the Eltham estates were inherited by various members of the de Clare and de Vesci families. In 1296 they were entrusted to Antony Bek, the Prince-Bishop of Durham. He carried out extensive building works to his home in Eltham, which he presented to Edward, Prince of Wales, who became King Edward II in 1307. Bishop Bek died at Eltham in 1311 and was taken with great ceremony for burial at Durham Cathedral. Bek's Eltham home was to become Eltham Palace. Much of the extensive land holdings around the palace remained in Crown ownership well into the 20th century.

In 1315 Michael of Canterbury was employed as designer and supervisor of a fence round the Manor of Eltham which created two parks known as the Great Park and Middle Park. Horne Park was the result of a further enclosure some 150 years later. These enclosures were reserved for hunting by royal parties. Deer bones were discovered during an archaeological dig at Middle Park Farmhouse in 1972.

Edward II's second son, John, was born at Eltham Palace in 1316 and became known as John of Eltham. His early death in 1336 at Perth was caused by a fever which he contracted while on a fighting campaign against the Scots. He was buried in Westminster Abbey. On the 650th anniversary of his birth in 1966 flowers were taken from Eltham Palace and placed on his tomb. This commemoration is continued annually by local schoolchildren under the sponsorship of the Eltham Society.

In the 14th century Eltham became a royal residence of great importance. Meetings of Parliament were held there and tournaments staged within the walls of the Tilt Yard. In 1347 at the tournament celebrating victory at the Battle of Crécy it is considered that the Order of the Garter was first seen in public as attested by the Royal Wardrobe Accounts for 1347: 'For making twelve garters of blue, embroidered with gold and silk each having a motto "Honi soit qui mal y pense" and for making other equipment for the King's joust at Eltham ...'.

Geoffrey Chaucer, the writer and poet, was Clerk of the Works at Eltham and other royal palaces. In 1390 while returning to Eltham from Westminster with pay for his workmen he was robbed of £10 at Hatcham, New Cross. The hapless man was waylaid again at the same spot when he returned with fresh wages but this time the thieves also took his horse. Chaucer was dismissed in 1391.

2 The moat bridge at Eltham Palace in 1820.

Christmas was celebrated in 1482 by Edward IV with great style. Some two thousand people were entertained and the food required included: peacocks, 4,000; quails, 2,400; capons, 2,000; swans, 2,000; kids, 2,000; plovers, 1,200; sheep, 1,000; geese, 1,000; pigs, 800; calves, 304; bulls, 6. This was followed by 4,000 dishes of jelly and 2,000 portions of hot custard.

Towards the end of Edward's reign in 1482 the rebuilding of the moat bridge and the Great Hall were completed. This fine building, topped with its chestnut hammerbeam roof, and the bridge are the only surviving structures for us to enjoy today.

Henry VII and Henry VIII made improvements to their palace at Eltham including the rebuilding of the chapel. Cardinal Wolsey was created Lord Chancellor of England in 1515 at Eltham and stayed at accommodation just outside the moat now known as Lord Chancellor's Lodgings. Eltham had reached the zenith of its royal patronage. Henry VIII was turning his attention to other royal palaces like those at Greenwich and Hampton Court and Eltham's importance waned.

A surviving building from these times is the Tudor Barn at Well Hall Pleasaunce. It stands alongside a moat which surrounds a piece of level land where once stood a building considered to be of Tudor origin. The brick bridge which gives access to the site is probably of the same age. The initials 'WR' on brickwork at the side of the Tudor Barn are those of William Roper whose family owned the estates at Well Hall for many generations. His wife Margaret was the daughter of Henry VIII's former Lord Chancellor, Sir Thomas More, who was beheaded by the King in 1535. A date plaque of 1568 is attached to an outer wall of the Tudor Barn. The derelict barn was restored in 1936 by Woolwich Borough Council for use as a restaurant and art gallery but was closed by Greenwich Council in 1993 as an economy measure. It reopened in 1995 as a restaurant and bar.

Eltham in medieval times has been recalled by William Shakespeare in his play *King Henry VI*. In Act I scene i occurs this reference:

> Exeter: To Eltham will I, where the young king is,
> Being ordain'd his special governor;
> And for his safety there I'll best devise

> Winchester: Each hath his place and function to attend:
> I am left out; for me nothing remains.
> But long I will no be Jack-out-of-office
> The king from Eltham I intend to steal
> And sit at chiefest stern of public weal.

During the Civil War in the 17th century many of Eltham's trees were felled and taken to Deptford and Woolwich where they were used for shipbuilding. The former wooded areas were turned over to farming which altered the landscape in these parts. Peace brought prosperity and after the restoration of the monarchy in 1660 the manor of Eltham was granted by Charles II to Sir John Shaw who had given him financial support during his exile. As the former palace was in a ruinous state he decided to build himself a new home in a contemporary style on the site of a keeper's lodge in the Great Park. After visiting the site in 1664 the diarist John Evelyn wrote: 'Thence to Eltham to see Sir John Shaw's new house now building, the place is pleasant, if not too wett, but the house is not well contrived, especially the roofe and dormers too low pitched, and kitchens where the cellars should be'.

3 The six original Thomas Philipot almshouses were built in 1694 at Eltham High Street. They stood between *The Rising Sun* public house and Blunts Road.

The house, Eltham Lodge, has been the headquarters of the Royal Blackheath Golf Club since 1923, following an amalgamation with the Eltham Golf Club, who had been using the house and grounds since 1892.

Thomas Philipot inherited land at Eltham, Footscray and Sidcup from his father John Philipot. Following the death of Thomas in 1682 six almshouses 'for poore people' were erected in 1694 according to instructions in his will. They were built in the High Street and survived until 1929 when they were demolished for road widening. The replacement almshouses can be seen in Philipot Path. In 1738, near to the Philipot Almshouses, was erected the Eltham Workhouse. It opened a year later and provided accommodation, food and clothing for the poor of the parish.

Most of the inhabitants of Eltham lived in the vicinity of the High Street which was on the route to and from London and Kent. Wealthy people who settled in Eltham built large detached houses with extensive rear walled gardens. A surviving example is Cliefden House (c.1720) and

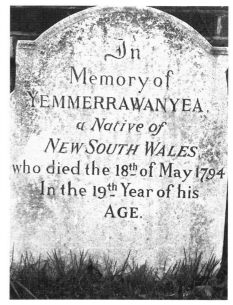

4 The tombstone of Yemmerrawanyea in St John's churchyard. It stands by the footpath which leads from the church lych-gate to Well Hall Road.

its stable block to the rear. This house, which stands opposite Passey Place, is now used for shops and offices and its former garden has been built on. The modest cottages of the less wealthy inhabitants have not survived as they have been demolished in the course of progress. However, births, marriages, deaths and possibly any fineable misdemeanours survive in the parish records of St John's Church. The earliest surviving Parish Account book is from 1554. Although the present church only dates back to the 1870s, there has been a church here for over nine hundred years; the first known priest was Adam de Bromleigh in 1160. Many of the inhabitants of Eltham are buried in the extensive churchyard which is now closed for new burials. In 1794 an Australian aborigine died at Eltham while visiting this country. Yemmerrawanyea Kebbarah was buried in the churchyard and his tombstone is a subject of much interest. Thomas Doggett (1650-1721) is remembered as the founder, in 1715, of the river Thames boat race which bears his name. He lived his last years in Eltham and a memorial plaque can be seen on the outer south wall of the church. Another colourful character who lived at Eltham in his final years was John Lilburne (1614-57). Known as 'Free-born John', he was a political agitator and caused problems for King Charles I and Cromwell. He died in Eltham but was buried at Moorfields, London. His memory survives as a local road name.

There is reference to a school, and the master 'Old Wybourne', in the early 17th century. It was improved in 1634 and was thought to be near St John's Church. In 1814 the church built a National School at Pound Place (now the site of Kwiksave) for £820. A National Infants School was built nearby at Back Lane (now Philipot Path) in 1852; the building was used by St Mary's School until 1984 when it was bought by J. Sainsbury.

The Eltham National School was relocated to Roper Street in 1868 and is now known as Eltham Church of England School. Mr. R.R.C. Gregory was the headmaster from 1901-20 and in 1909 his book *The Story of Royal Eltham* was published. This book gives the first comprehensive account of Eltham's history and is supported by photographs which give a glimpse of the village days which were soon to vanish.

Mr. Thomas Chester Haworth (1815-87) came to Eltham in 1839 as a tailor. He later became an estate agent, property developer, newspaper owner, and surveyor for Eltham. In the latter position he organised the change from cess-pits to main drainage. As a man of independent principles he objected to being buried in the churchyard at St John's and received permission to construct his own family mausoleum at Mottingham which survives at Beaconsfield Road. The West Kent sewer was constructed in New Eltham under a statute of 1875 but the connection to local houses took some years to complete.

The Eltham Gas Light and Coke Company Ltd. was formed in 1852 and the gas works was sited off the High Street near the present Arcade. About 1858 the company built larger premises for the manufacture of gas at Eltham Green but was taken over by the Phoenix Company in 1876. The premises were used as a council yard until 1933 when they were relocated to Sun Yard, Archery Road.

The population of Eltham and Mottingham in 1801 was 1,702 but had more than doubled to 2,568 by 1851. The census for 1881 records a further doubling of the population to 5,827. The increase in population was principally due to the building of new housing following the construction of the Dartford Loop railway line. The line was constructed almost a mile to the south of the High Street and was opened on 1 September 1866 with passenger facilities provided at Eltham station (now Mottingham). Pope Street station (now New Eltham) on the same line was not opened until 1878. The original settlement of Mottingham, along Mottingham Lane, was extended into what is now known as Mottingham village by the building of houses, shops and community facilities following the opening of the railway connection with London. Development at New Eltham followed a similar pattern.

The Crown granted 99-year building leases on its land at Eltham. Some detached houses that have had their leases extended can still be seen in Court Road and Wythfield Road. Large houses built at North Park in the 1860s were replaced by flats at Greenacres and Woodington Close as the leases expired. The construction of Marlowe Gardens by Rush and Tompkins in 1978 replaced four detached and two semi-detached houses which fronted Eltham High Street and were contemporary with the extant Eltham Conservative Club premises.

Since its demise as a royal residence Eltham Palace has suffered much neglect and spoilation. The Great Hall became a barn and together with the surviving buildings was known as Court Farm. The 'ruins' were visited by antiquarians and artists like Paul Sandby and J.M.W. Turner. Some artists' graphic representations were of a highly romantic nature. Mr. R. Bloxham became a Crown tenant in 1859 and moved the farming activities to the presently named King John's Walk. He instigated building works and other improvements which transformed the former farm and yard into a gentleman's residence which he renamed Eltham Court. The Great Hall became an indoor tennis court.

Eltham was becoming the home for people with national connections who no doubt found the country air quite favourable. The Goschen family moved from Stoke

5 This print was published in 1820 and is entitled 'Remains of Eltham Palace, Kent'.

Newington in the 1830s to a house in the High Street that is now the St Mary's Community Centre. After his marriage in 1859 their son William lived at Eagle House in the High Street (now Christchurch Priory). He was elected M.P. for the City of London and achieved high political office including that of Chancellor of the Exchequer. In 1900 he was created Viscount Goschen of Hawkhurst.

Eltham became embroiled in political scandal following the disclosure that one of its residents, Mrs. Katherine O'Shea, was having an affair with M.P. Charles Stewart Parnell who led the (Irish) Home Rule party at Westminster. He made clandestine visits to her home at North Park and the newspapers were soon on his trail. Parnell fell from power and the cause of Irish Home Rule was delayed for many years. After the O'Sheas divorced, Katherine married Parnell but he died a few months later in 1891.

Colonel North, who made his fortune principally by exploiting the nitrate fields of Chile and became known as the 'Nitrate King', purchased Avery Hill in 1882. His architect, T.W. Cutler, replaced a modest house with a mansion of 50 rooms which was surrounded by a coach house, paddock, stables and pleasure gardens. The work took eight years to complete and became the centre of lavish entertainment. Colonel North died in 1896 and is buried at St John's churchyard.

Between 1884 and 1885 the naturalist and writer, Richard Jefferies, and his family lived at 14 Victoria Road. In 1986 a Greater London Council Blue Plaque was unveiled at their former home, now 59 Footscray Road.

As Eltham developed there was pressure to build Anglican churches to serve the new communities. This could only be achieved by reducing the acreage of the parish of St John's church. The new parishes and their churches were: Christ Church, Shooters

6 Colonel North's mansion at Avery Hill in 1908. It was bought by the London County Council in 1902 and in 1906 became Avery Hill College where female teachers were trained. The college facilities are now part of the University of Greenwich.

Hill (1864); Holy Trinity, Southend Crescent (1869); St Peter, Lee (1871); St Andrew, Mottingham (1880); All Saints, New Eltham (1898; as a separate parish from Holy Trinity in 1929); St Luke, Westmount Road (1907); St Barnabas, Rochester Way (1933); St Saviour, Middle Park Avenue (1933); St Edward the Confessor, Keverne Road, Mottingham (1958).

The first post-Reformation Roman Catholic church, St Mary's, was erected in the High Street in 1890 next to the building now known as the St Mary's Community Centre. A larger building, Christ Church, was erected further along the High Street in 1912. The other local Catholic churches are Our Lady Help of Christians, Mottingham Road (1933), St Thomas More, Well Hall Road (1936), and St Bernadette, Middle Park Avenue (1939).

Non-Conformist congregations have had a strong presence in Eltham. The Eltham United Reformed church originates from a late 18th-century foundation. A permanent church, built in 1839 on the site of the present Arcade, was replaced by a new larger church in 1846 on land owned by Mr. Henry Dobell and now the site of the McDonalds restaurant. The present premises in Court Road were completed in 1936. The Methodist tradition can be traced back to the Bible Christians who worshipped in a chapel in Elizabeth Terrace—a stone from this building has been fitted into a wall at the Eltham Park Methodist church (founded 1902, church opened 1906). The New Eltham Methodist church was opened in 1958 and replaced a timber and asbestos building of 1930. The Rev. Charles Wesley was obviously not impressed by his visit to Eltham as he recorded in his diary for 16 June 1740 that he was taken to King John's chapel (Eltham Palace) where 'Several of the assembly-ladies heard me patiently, while I showed them they were in no wise better than the harlots and publicans.'

The Strict Baptists acquired part of a former brewery for their meetings in 1883. In 1904 they moved from the High Street to a larger church at Balkaskie Road. The Eltham Park Baptist Church opened in 1912 and the first house meeting was held 10 years earlier.

More change came to the area following the completion of the Bexleyheath railway line through Well Hall and Eltham Park in 1895. Well Hall station was opened on 1 May 1895. The opening of Shooters Hill station (later Eltham Park) was delayed until 1 July 1908 due to a lengthy legal case concerning the closure of Well Hall station.

Just north of the railway line at Well Hall stood Well Hall House. From 1899 it became the home of the Bland family. Mrs. Bland is better-known as Edith Nesbit the author of children's books, *The Railway Children* and *The Treasure Seekers*, both written at Well Hall. The site of her house, by the Tudor Barn, is now part of Well Hall Pleasaunce.

The famous cricketer W.G. Grace moved to Fairmount, Mottingham Lane in 1909. He continued to use his cricket skills as a member of the Eltham Cricket Club and in his last match scored 69 not out against Grove Park. He died at Fairmount in 1915 and is buried at Elmers End cemetery, Beckenham.

Most local jobs have been concerned with servicing the needs of the local community or with farming until the farms disappeared. There is record of Gathercole's Envelope Factory in the mid-1850s, while at the end of the 19th century Gilbert Whitehead established a printing works at Hainault Street, New Eltham. The navigational instrument makers, Heath & Co. Ltd., relocated from Crayford to New Eltham in 1916. They amalgamated with W.F. Stanley in 1926 and the business survives today. Walter Grafton started his Eltham business in temporary buildings by Well Hall station in 1913. His company was registered in 1914 and five years later moved to a new factory in Footscray Road. The company eventually employed over 300 men and women who produced spools for typewriters, cash registers and computers. Nearly 700 varieties of spools were manufactured and 60 per cent were exported. B & Q opened a store on the site of the factory in 1988.

In 1900 Cameron Corbett started building houses on the land he had bought at Well Hall and Eltham Park. The roads were laid out mainly to a grid pattern, as can be seen at Corbett's other estates at

7   Dr. W.G. Grace at his home Fairmount, Mottingham Lane. A London Blue Plaque was unveiled here in 1966 to commemorate his residence at the house.

Hither Green and Ilford. Names with Scottish associations were given to the roads. Corbett was an M.P. for Glasgow and in 1911 was created the first Baron Rowallan. Building work stopped in 1914 at the commencement of the First World War. Bob Hope was born at no. 44 Craigton Road on 29 May 1903 in a house built by his grandfather's firm, Picton and Hope. Charles Folkard, the artist who invented the children's cartoon strip character 'Teddy Tail of the Daily Mail'—the mouse with the top hat—lived at no. 2 Balcaskie Road. He had the inspiration for the character on his way home to Eltham by train in 1915.

A tram service from Woolwich to Eltham started in 1910. The trams terminated at Well Hall Road by St John's Church on a new stretch of road which had been constructed between the railway bridge at Well Hall and the High Street in 1905. The existence of this tram route was a prime consideration in siting a new estate for Woolwich Arsenal munition workers at Well Hall. The estate was designed on garden city lines and work commenced early in 1915. By the end of the year nearly 1,300 houses and some flats had been built on either side of Well Hall Road on 96 acres of former farmland. The estate was bought by the Royal Arsenal Co-operative Society in 1925 and named the Progress Estate.

On the uncompleted sections of the Corbett Estate temporary wooden detached hutments were erected in 1916 to house more munition workers and their families. Other sites were also used for this type of housing and a total of 1,500 hutments were erected in Eltham—the largest such concentration in the country. Former residents include politician Lord Healey, and comedian Frankie Howerd. Some of these temporary homes survived until 1935 when the last tenants were rehoused. Morrell Builders Ltd.

8 Ross Way, part of the Well Hall Estate which was built in 1915 for munition workers at the Royal Arsenal at Woolwich. The area is now known as the Progress Estate and in 1971 was designated as a Conservation Area by the Department of the Environment.

replaced huts with houses on the slopes of Shooters Hill behind the *Welcome Inn* public house; likewise Percy Bilton (Eltham) Ltd. completed the Corbett Estate with different styles of housing.

Woolwich Borough Council's Page Estate was started in 1920 and by 1930 houses had been built from Eltham Hill to Rochester Way. Schools, shops, open spaces and churches were all included in the scheme. Middle Park Farm and part of Horn Park Farm were sold by the Crown to Woolwich Borough Council so that permanent housing could be provided for the tenants from the Eltham hutments. Cottage-type houses and flats were built together with provision for community facilities and good allocations of open space. The London County Council bought farmland at Mottingham for a new housing estate which opened in 1935. Over 2,000 dwellings were built in addition to shops, schools, churches and a pub. Houses for purchase were built by Barwells, Davis Estates, W. Scudamore and Wates at New Eltham.

In 1933 the Crown granted a lease to Stephen Courtauld for Eltham Palace and 50 acres of land. The fields around the palace were preserved from building and still maintain a rural air astride King John's Walk. Stephen Courtauld removed the Victorian buildings from the palace site and erected a new home in their place which was named Eltham Hall. He also spent much money on restoring the Great Hall and it is a credit to him that the building survives today. He surrendered his lease in 1944 and a year later the Army Education Corps moved in. Due to reductions in funding the Ministry of Defence decided to relocate its education services and withdrew from Eltham Palace in 1992. A new tenant is awaited.

9 Eltham Hall at Eltham Palace was completed for Stephen Courtauld in 1936. The architects were the Honourable John Seeley (later Lord Mottistone) and Paul Paget.

Eltham's location near to London made it almost inevitable that it would be affected by aerial bombardment in the Second World War. Much damage occurred during the Battle of Britain in 1940 but worse was to come in the shape of the V1 and V2 attacks in 1944 and 1945. St Barnabas's Church was wrecked by indendiary bombs in 1944. In the same year a V1 flying bomb caused severe damage to Hitches garage and made the top of the spire fall from St John's Church in the High Street.

The shortage of post-war housing was eased by the construction of pre-fabs on bomb sites, vacant land and at public parks like Eltham Park South. Eltham's last remaining large farm, at Coldharbour, was bought from the Crown by Woolwich Borough Council and house building started in 1947. At Avery Hill London County Council completed a building scheme that was started just before the Second World War.

The need to move traffic between London and the Kent coastal ports has meant that Eltham could not avoid taking its share of major roads. The opening of the Eltham By Pass (now the A20, Sidcup Road) in 1923 routed traffic away from a High Street that still resembled, in places, a village street. The completion of the Rochester Way (the A2) as a London radial route in the early 1930s brought more traffic into residential areas that were not designed to cope with such flows. Living with the increased levels of traffic became intolerable. After much public protest the Greater London Council agreed to build the Rochester Way Relief Road. The completed road was opened by local M.P. Peter Bottomley in 1988 and is now the A2.

The major development of Eltham from a Kentish village to a suburb of London has been accomplished in about 150 years. One wonders whether the next 150 years will see such dramatic change and Eltham will still be a home worth returning to.

Eltham Palace

10 The Great Hall was built by King Edward IV and completed in 1480. It is the only building surviving from the former royal palace at Eltham. This view shows the south side of the Great Hall with the Victorian residence built by Mr. Bloxham to the right.

11 The north side of the Great Hall in 1904. There was no glass in the windows at this time due to poor maintenance of the building.

12 The magnificent chestnut hammerbeam roof of the Great Hall can be seen in this picture of 1906. The floor is marked out for use as an indoor tennis court, an improvement on its previous use as a barn.

13 Mr. R. Bloxham leased Eltham Palace from the Crown in 1859. From a collection of decaying buildings previously used as Court Farm he created a comfortable country retreat by adding a new residence which he named Eltham Court.

14 Mr. Bloxham was a keen supporter of the local volunteer force and allowed them to muster at Eltham Palace. This rare picture shows a uniformed member of the Eltham Volunteer Regiment, the 32nd Kent (Eltham) Corps., Sergeant Isaac Wilkins, at a summer camp in 1870 with members of his family. The Wilkins family lived nearby at no.5 Wellington Road (now the site of Ruskin Court, Wythfield Road).

15 The Eltham Rose Show notice, 1910.

16 Across the medieval bridge, reflected in the moat, can be seen the Moat House built in 1859 by Richard Bloxham.

17 The programme cover for the May Fayre at Eltham Palace in 1924 was designed by Charles Folkard.

18 The Great Hall as restored by Stephen Courtauld in 1936. Two episodes of the B.B.C. programme Mastermind were recorded in the hall on 10 December 1986.

19 The main entrance to Eltham Hall as built by Stephen Courtauld. Two of the three Tudor gables which were incorporated into the work can be seen in this picture taken in the 1950s. The six roof finials depict chess pieces.

20 The Great Hall and dry moat in 1964. The foundations of the royal kitchens survive under the grass in front of these buildings.

21 The Queen visited Eltham Palace in 1970 for the 50th anniversary of the Royal Army Education Corps., based at Eltham Palace from 1945 to 1992. The Queen can be seen in her car at Court Yard on the journey home.

22 An inadequate supply of water at Eltham Palace prompted the construction of an underground conduit, laid across the Great Park to a source at the Warren, Gravel Pit Lane. An old conduit head can be seen alongside the footpath at Holy Trinity Church in Southend Crescent. This postcard, dated 1912, shows the conduit head and the detached Rusthall Lodge, which is now used by the Greenwich Health Authority.

23 A range of buildings outside the moat at Eltham Palace was used for such purposes as a coal store, spicery, bakehouse and a candlehouse (or chaundry). The houses in this picture were used as the residence of the Lord Chancellor when staying at Eltham Palace. They were restored in 1951 and are now private residences.

24 The rear of the Chancellor's Lodgings in 1905 when the Tudor construction had been obliterated by Kentish weatherboarding.

Historic Buildings

25 Well Hall House stood in the grounds of the present Well Hall Pleasaunce between Well Hall Road and the moat. The Roper estates at Well Hall were sold to Sir Gregory Page of Blackheath in 1733 who had this house built. Nothing survives of the medieval house which was surrounded by the moat. Between 1899 and 1922 Well Hall House was the home of the Bland family. Mrs. Bland was widely known as Edith Nesbit, author of many famous children's stories including *The Railway Children* and *The Treasure Seekers*, which were written whilst she lived at Eltham.

26 Sherard House in the High Street was named after the famous botanists Dr. James and Dr. William Sherard who lived here in the 18th century. Mr. Henry Dobell lived here with his family from 1857 until his death in 1895 and is remembered in a local road name. The National Westminster Bank stands on part of the site of Sherard House and opened on 3 January 1922.

27 The rear of Sherard House, 1910. William Sherard wrote to a friend in 1725, 'My old gardener having left things in the utmost disorder, and my new one not understanding much of my garden, this pins me down, and obliges me not to stir from home this summer'.

28 Eltham Lodge, Court Road was built for Sir John Shaw by Hugh May in 1664 on part of the Royal Great Park. The Shaw family were Crown tenants until the early 19th century. Between 1838 and 1891 it was the home of Mrs. Anna Wood who was known as Aunt Ben by her niece Katherine O'Shea who lived nearby at North Park. The lease on the house and grounds was taken by the Eltham Golf Club in 1892 who amalgamated with the Royal Blackheath Golf Club in 1923 and remain on this site.

29 Severndroog Castle, Shooters Hill, 1910. This architectural folly was built to commemorate Sir William James. It has the same name as a building on the Malabar coast in India that was a pirate stronghold and was successfully attacked by James when working for the East India Company. The local castle was erected by his widow, Lady James, in 1784 and could be seen from her home, Park Farm Place, that stood on the site of St Mary's School, Glenure Road.

30 Sir William James, 1721-1783.

31 The Orangery, Orangery Lane. This 18th-century building stood at the end of the garden of Eltham House (*see* no.160) and has now been marooned between a public footpath and the Marks and Spencer car park. This picture shows construction of the access road for the Merlewood telephone exchange in 1971. The Orangery still awaits sympathetic restoration.

32 Avery Hill College. This picture, dated 1912, shows the main entrance of 1890 to Colonel North's mansion at Avery Hill. Despite air-raid damage in the Second World War, this Victorian feature survives as part of the University of Greenwich.

33 The dining hall, Avery Hill College, 1910. The female students dined in Colonel North's former ballroom and picture gallery with the staff overseeing proceedings from the high table to the left of the picture. In 1993 the University of Greenwich restored the ceiling paintings when the hall was remodelled as a library.

Almshouses

34 The Fifteen Penny Land Charity dates back to 1492 when King Henry VII gave 38 acres of land in Eltham to the local people of Eltham to ensure, through the accrued revenues, that they could pay a tax called a fifteenth. In 1738 the Eltham Workhouse was built on part of that land called Blunts Croft which fronted the High Street. It can be seen at the centre of this picture of 1910 when it was known as the Fifteen Pennyland Almshouses and stood opposite the fire station. Note the speed limit of 10 m.p.h. and the contrasting attire of the two schoolboys.

35 Prior to demolition of the old almshouses in 1964 new accommodation was built nearby in Blunts Road on land owned by the Eltham United Charities. The 16 units of the Fifteen Penny Fields Almshouses were officially opened by Viscountess Davidson on 27 June 1963. The pavement water pump in the previous picture was externally restored in 1985 after spending many years in the gardens at Well Hall Pleasaunce. It stands on the lawn to the left of the main building in this picture taken in 1964.

36 The Forster Almshouses were built in 1711 at the end of a short yard by the side of the *White Hart* pub in the High Street. These buildings survived until the *White Hart* was rebuilt in 1926.

37 To the rear of the original Thomas Philipot Almshouses (no.3) in Blunts Road were built three extra units in 1872. The property was used as almshouses until 1968 when sold for private residential use. This picture of nos. 3, 5 and 7 Blunts Road was taken in 1965.

38 Six new almshouses were built for the Thomas Philipot Charity in 1929 to replace the 1694 building which was to be demolished for widening the High Street. The site at Back Lane, now Philipot Path, was formerly Lowaters Nursery. This picture, taken in 1965, shows the two blocks of almshouses with six and three units respectively. Subsequent building works have linked the two blocks and added further units and a hall to the site. The charity celebrated its 300th anniversary in 1994.

39 The original Geffrye Almshouses at Kingsland Road, London, E2 were established in 1714 with funds bequeathed by Sir Robert Geffrye, Master of the Ironmongers' Company in 1667 and 1685, and are now used as the Geffrye Museum. New almshouses, as seen here at Mottingham Road, were built by the Worshipful Company of Ironmongers amid open fields, in 1912, but are now in private residential use.

Churches

40 St John's Church in the High Street before being rebuilt in 1875. The new church incorporated the old tower and spire that can be seen in this picture. Note the water pump by the old wall and the entrance to the footpath which is still in use today.

41 The rebuilt St John's Church with the tower that was added in 1880.

42 A new vicarage was built in 1872 during the vicariate of the Rev. W.J. Sowerby. The name Sowerby Close has been given to the three blocks of flats built on the vicarage site in 1966.

43 St John's church hall, Wellington Road, was opened by the bishop of Southwark on 22 September 1910. It was used for church and community functions until 1946 when it was leased to Eltham Little Theatre Ltd. In 1982 the building was renamed as The Bob Hope Theatre in recognition of the financial assistance given to the theatre by Bob Hope.

44   The church of Holy Trinity, Southend Crescent, was built in 1869 to service the spiritual needs of this expanding area of Eltham. This picture, which includes the hall and vicarage, was taken before the church was extended towards the road in 1909. The Gallipoli Memorial Chapel was unveiled on 25 April 1917. Holy Trintity Church was chosen for this memorial as the vicar, the Rev. H. Hall, had been Divisional Chaplain to the 29th Division who fought at Gallipoli, Turkey, in 1915.

45   St Andrew's Church at Mottingham was consecrated in 1880. It was known as the 'church in the fields', as can be seen in this picture, until the 1930s when houses were built in Court Road.

46 St Peter's Church at The Avenue, now Courtlands Avenue, Lee was built in 1870. The church was damaged by enemy action during the Second World War and demolished in 1960. All that survives is a stone cross and commemorative plaque.

47 A new St Peter's Church and hall was built on land at the junction of Eltham Road and Weigall Road in 1960 in place of a wooden hut which had been used by the church since 1952. This picture was taken in 1981. A new church and some flats were built here in 1984.

48 The District Church of All Saints was built at Bercta Road, New Eltham, in 1898. This picture of 1905 shows the church with its 'tin' chancel and a wooden structure which housed the bell. All Saints was created a parish in 1929 with the Rev. A. Norledge as the first vicar. Building works in 1931 and 1937 enlarged the church to its present size.

49 St Barnabas Church, Rochester Way, was consecrated on 7 October 1933, but its story goes back to 1857 when it was built to the design of Sir Gilbert Scott as the Woolwich Dockyard church. As the building had become redundant at Woolwich, it was dismantled and removed to Eltham where it was erected as the permanent church of St Barnabas.

50 The interior of St Saviour's Church, Middle Park Avenue, designed by architects Welch, Cachemaille-Day and Lander in 1933.

51 St Alban's Church, Coldharbour, was consecrated in 1953 and funded with war damage money redirected from a church that was not rebuilt.

52 In 1910 Eagle House in the High Street was bought as a site for a new Roman Catholic church to replace the nearby smaller church of St Mary's. The house, in the centre of the picture, was renamed Christ Church Priory and a new church to the same dedication was built on part of the garden in 1912. The picture shows construction progress on a wing of the new Priory in 1964. For many years Robinsons Gardens leased land at the rear of the new building.

53 Since 1906 the Canons Regular of the Lateran have been responsible for the spiritual needs of the Roman Catholic community in Eltham and they are based at Christ Church Priory. This picture shows members of the team in the 1930s. Standing left to right: Fr. Bernard McKeon, Br. Anthony Fitzgerald, Fr. Reginald Vaughan, Fr. Leo Montgomery. Seated left to right: Prior Isidore O'Leary, Abbot Augustine White, Fr. Leo Holden.

54 The Eltham Congregational Church in 1912 at the junction of the High Street and Well Hall Road. The church was built in 1868 on land given by Mr. H. Dobell, McDonalds now operates from the building on this site, built for Burtons after the church moved to Court Road in 1936.

55 The Eltham Baptist Meeting Room was above the stables of a building that was formerly the Eltham Brewery. The site is now part of Allders car park.

56 In 1904 the Baptist congregation moved to a permanent building at Balcaskie Road which was known as the Eltham Baptist church. The building was sold in 1958 and houses were built on the site. The picture shows the church in 1904.

57 The Eltham Park Methodist Church, Westmount Road, opened for worship in 1906 and was originally known as the Walford Green Memorial Church. Earlier services had been held in a temporary iron building. This picture shows the newly-built church alongside Earshall Road and a milk pram from Howes Dairy.

58 The Eltham Park Baptist Church in 1916, four years after it opened. The building on the right was opened in 1903 as a school chapel. Badly damaged in the Second World War, as was the church, a newly-built hall was completed in 1958.

Public Houses

59 & 60 (*above and opposite*) The licence for the *Castle Inn*, High Street, had recently been transferred to Mr. W. Parker when these photos were taken in 1903. The premises were rebuilt in 1905 and again in 1962.

61 The *Rising Sun* is the only pub on the north side of the High Street. This picture of 1900 shows the original pub before being demolished to make way for a civic development by Woolwich Borough Council; only the library was built. The present pub, further up the High Street, opened in 1904 with Mr. W. Relf as the licensee. The name 'Sun Yard' for Greenwich Council's depot at Archery Road reminds us of the former pub yard which stood on this site.

62 The *Greyhound c.*1904, when the licensee was Henry Elms who came to Eltham in 1897 from the *Three Blackbirds* at Blendon, Kent. Jack Elms kept up the family connection with the *Greyhound* until his death in 1970. In this picture a workman is removing part of the pub roof in connection with work to widen the access between Mellins and the pub to ensure that the Tillings horse bus, used on the Eltham to Blackheath service, could be stabled at the rear.

63 A Beasleys horse-drawn delivery cart stands outside the *Crown*, Court Yard, in 1906 after its journey from the company's North Kent Brewery at Plumstead. Despite the name of the pub, the site was not owned by the Crown but, at that time, by the Thomas Philipot Charity. The pub was rebuilt in 1930.

64 Perhaps the driver of the horse-drawn cart is testing the offerings of the Dartford Brewery Co. in the *White Hart* at no. 2 High Street. The pub was rebuilt in 1926.

65 The *Chequers* pub, as seen here, was rebuilt in 1904 and set back across the pavement. Note the unusual finials to the gables and the old milestone on the pavement.

66 The *Royal Hotel*, Court Road, was built following the opening of Eltham station in 1866. A new pub of the same name, was opened nearby at Sidcup Road in 1934. The flats of Royal Court stand on the site of the old pub. The picture was taken *c.*1910.

67 The *Porcupine* at Mottingham, *c*.1914. The trough by the pavement provided a useful water supply for horses belonging to the Royal Artillery who came here from Woolwich to exercise with draghounds over the local farms.

68 The *Porcupine* was rebuilt in 1922 after the old wooden pub was pulled down with the help of a traction engine. The picture on this postcard was drawn by Eltham artist Llwyd Roberts. The message on the back reads: 'WVS [Womens' Voluntary Service]. Owing to frequent air-raids the meetings at the Porcupine are postponed until further notice. Work will be received and given out at 2 Court Farm Road on Wednesdays and Fridays from 10.30-12.30'. No. 2 Court Farm Road was the home of Mr. and Mrs. Charles Folkard.

69 The *King and Queen*, Kimmeridge Road, was built about 1937 to serve the residents of the new Mottingham Estate. This picture, taken in 1983, shows the front of the pub closed by Trumans in 1992 and demolished for a housing development which bears the name King and Queen Close.

70 The *Beehive* at New Eltham was built in 1897 and replaced an earlier pub. Mr. M. Choppin became licensee in 1926 after moving from the *Man of Kent* in the High Street. The family connection continued until his son Bob Choppin retired in 1973.

Farming and Countryside

71 St John's Church, 1847. The two cows are resting by a footpath, replaced by Well Hall Road. One of the Church Yard Cottages, on the left of the picture, was the birthplace of George Marks in 1858. On his elevation to the peerage in 1929 he took the title (The First) Baron Marks of Woolwich. The cottages would have stood in front of the present police station and were demolished when the new road was constructed in 1905.

72 Pippenhall Farm, Bexley Road, 1912. Members of the Grace family farmed here in Victorian times and into the 20th century. Horses are now stabled where the old farm buildings once stood alongside Butterfly Lane.

73 Crown Woods Lane, 1930. In 1934 J. Webb & Co. started to build the Eltham Heights Estate which transformed this lane into Crown Woods Way. This cottage survived until the Second World War (see no.117).

74 Avery Hill Road on the way to the junction with Halfway Street in the early 1920s. This rural scene disappeared a few years later when new houses and bungalows were constructed alongside a widened stretch of new road.

75 Pope Street Dairy, Avery Hill Road. The farmhouse, known as Keightley House, stood near the present Keightley Drive and records the old name of this road and the district—Pope Street. Mr. Richard Pace, dairyman, managed the farm when this picture was taken *c.*1900.

76 This picture is titled 'Green Lane Farm, Southend' and was taken in the 1920s. Henry Furber was the dairyman here in 1920.

77 Chapel Farm, Mottingham, 1932. Most of the lane from Eltham to Chapel Farm was widened following the construction of the Dartford Loop railway in 1866 and renamed Court Road. The farm was owned by the Crown and in 1920 Haydn Fisher lived in the farmhouse. In the four cottages, with their families, lived Edward Cutmore, Harry Cutmore, William Dymott and William Walker.

78 To the south of Chapel Farm stood Coldharbour Farm which was also owned by the Crown until sold to Woolwich Borough Council in 1946. This picture shows haymaking near Coldharbour farmhouse in 1940. The cluster of farm buildings stood at the side of Mottingham Road almost opposite Elmstead Lane.

79 Acquisition of smaller dairy businesses by larger companies like the Express Dairy and United Dairies extended their network into suburban areas. This Express Dairy shop, pictured in the mid-1920s, stood next to the *Porcupine* pub at Mottingham. A milk distribution depot was later built on this site by the Express Dairy and used until closure in 1985. A dairy herd was kept at Mottingham Farm by the Express Dairy until the 1950s; the buildings are now used as a horse-riding centre.

80 Eltham Hill, just past Eltham Green, in 1906. A hay cart has stopped by the side of Lyme Farm on the road to Eltham. To the right of the brick walls and gardens in the centre of the picture stand four detached Victorian houses which were replaced by terrace houses in the early 1960s.

81 Farm workers at Lyme Farm in the 1920s. Harry Churchill, nephew of farmer Mr. W.F. Corp, is holding a sheep as the workers take a rest in the farmyard. The farmland stretched from Eltham Hill to the railway embankment and was bought by Woolwich Borough Council in 1919 to build the Page Estate. The Eltham Hill Working Men's Club was built on the site of the farmhouse of Lyme Farm in 1927.

Housing

82 An old cottage in Ram Alley, High Street, 1905. On the site of this cottage and Jubilee Cottages (following illustration) stands the Allders store.

83 Jubilee Cottages were built in 1833 and named in commemoration of the Rev. J. K. Shawbrooke's 50 years as vicar of St John's Church. This picture from 1910 catches a lady cleaning the front step.

84 Elm Terrace looking towards the High Street and the Philipot Almshouses in 1910. The cottages on the left were demolished for the Arcade development (1930) which was only half completed when the developer went bankrupt. The Elm Terrace Fitness Centre (opened in 1931 as an indoor market) covers the site of most of the cottages on the right except the last three, which are now used for commercial purposes.

85 (*above*) This postcard was sent from 9 Clarence Road, Mottingham, on 1 January 1918. The young lads in military uniform probably missed their chance to serve in the First World War as it was drawing to a close. A lady is delivering the post. All the houses shown here in Clarence Road were damaged and demolished following an air raid in the Second World War. The replacement flats are known as John Hunt Court.

86 (*above*) Court Farm Road, Mottingham, 1917. Note the man in military uniform and the milk delivery pram.

87 (*left*) Well Hall Road, 1912. The completion of this stretch of new road between the railway bridge at Well Hall and the High Street in 1905 enabled these houses, known as Spencer Gardens, to be built by W.C. Brake *c.*1906.

88 It is difficult to realise that this quiet scene at Deansfield Road, taken around 1910, is now the busy Rochester Way near its junction with Westmount Road. The policeman on horseback is patrolling through the newly built Corbett Estate. The houses on the left were destroyed by enemy action in the Second World War and replaced by post-war prefabs, and in the 1970s by the Garnett Close flats.

89 Elderslie Road in 1914, on the Corbett Estate. Note the iron gates and railings and young lime trees in the gardens. Many of the houses in this picture were destroyed in the Second World War and have been replaced by flats.

90 & 91 These two pictures taken from 63 Craigton Road, on the Corbett Estate, record the transformation that took place when the Progress Estate was built in 1915. The first view shows open land stretching across Well Hall Road in the direction of Kidbrooke. The second picture shows houses for munition workers under construction in Admiral Seymour Road. The greenhouse appears in both pictures.

92 To provide additional housing for Woolwich Arsenal munition workers, temporary dwellings, or hutments, were constructed in 1916 at Eltham Park and Well Hall. A few of these 1,500 hutments are shown here at Pellett Place with the woods of Shooters Hill as a backdrop. This location today would be near the roundabout at Westmount Road.

93 Woolwich Borough Council's Page Estate was built at Lyme Farm between 1920 and 1930. This view shows the houses and green at Philippa Gardens in 1930.

KEM ESTATE

FROM £885

'COMPLETE WITH GARAGE

BUILT-IN VACUUM CLEANER INSTALLATION

NO ROAD OR PAVING CHARGES.

Ideally situated with permanent open spaces—at Cedarhurst Drive, between the Eltham Road and the Sidcup Arterial Road, and only 18 minutes to London Bridge from Kidbrooke Southern Electric Station. Buses 21 and 132 and Trams 46 and 72 pass the Estate.

The houses are spacious and well built, only the finest materials having been used in their construction, the timber throughout being Pine and all floors are tongued and grooved.

Centro Vac Installation with motor and dust trap in cupboard under the stairs whereby every room is vacuum cleaned by just plugging into a point—no machine to carry.

3 LARGE BEDROOMS 15′ 6″ × 13′ 6″, 13′ 6″ × 13′ 6″ and 10′ × 10′

2 RECEPTION ROOMS 15′ 6″ (excluding bay) × 13′ 6″ and 15′ × 12′ 6″.

8′ wide HALL. TILED BATHROOM and KITCHEN with ample cupboard room throughout. Flush panel doors. **BRICK BUILT GARAGE.**

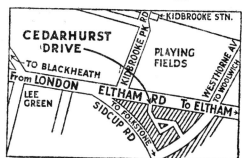

KEM ESTATES, LTD., CEDARHURST DRIVE, ELTHAM, S.E.9.

'Phone: Eltham 2876.

94 Kem Estate publicity, 1935.

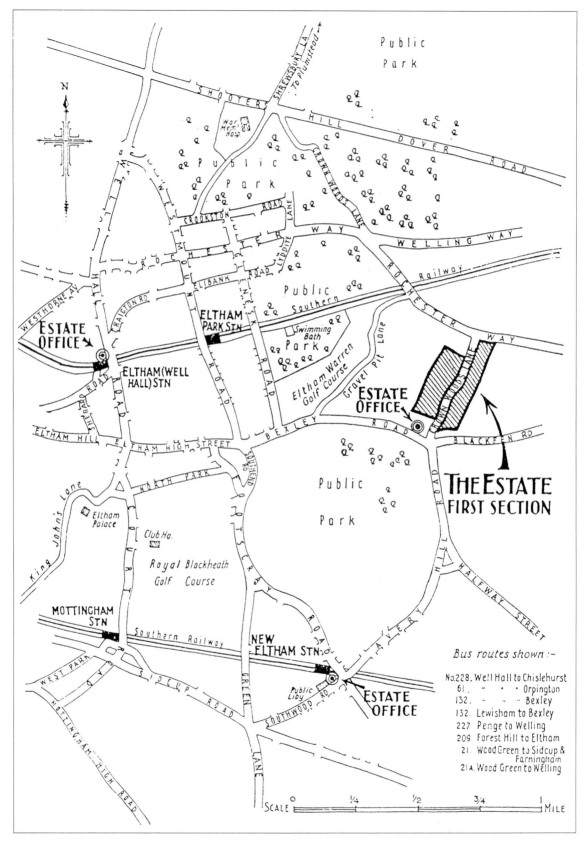

95 Location map for the Eltham Heights Estate, 1935.

"ELTHAM HEIGHTS"
TYPE "C"

PRICE £925   £70 CASH and 26/5 per week

NO LEGAL COSTS, STAMP DUTIES, MORTGAGE CHARGES OR SURVEY FEE.

NO ROAD OR PAVING CHARGES.

GROUND RENT (according to size of plot) from £8 18 6 per annum.

Charmingly designed in the "TUDOR STYLE." A really spacious Four-Bedroom "Family" House, with BRICK GARAGE in main building.

An imposing elevation, beautifully harmonising the beauties of "warm" brickwork, "half-timbering," bright stucco and mellow leaded window lights. With an enchanting oriel bay window beneath a bold gable and a tiled hood over entrance.

BEDROOM 1 - - - - - 16′ 0″ × 12′ 1½″	DINING ROOM - - - - - 14′ 0″ × 12′ 6″
BEDROOM 2 - - - - - 14′ 0″ × 12′ 6″	KITCHENETTE - - - - - 10′ 9″ × 10′ 6″
BEDROOM 3 - - - - - 12′ 1½″ × 10′ 10½″	BRICK GARAGE, with Brick Fuel Store
BEDROOM 4 - - - - - 14′ 0″ × 8′ 9″	at rear - - - - - 15′ 9″ × 7′ 6″ (inside)
HALL - - - - - - 6′ 4½″ wide.	
RECEPTION ROOM - - - - 16′ 0″ × 12′ 1½″	TRADE PORCH.

HAVE "AVERY HILL" PARK AT YOUR DOORSTEP

96 Details of an Eltham Heights house type, 1935.

97 These post-war prefabs were built on the site of bombed property at the junction of Green Lane and Parkview Road. A children's home was built here in 1972. It was replaced by the flats of Links Court in 1995.

98 This picture shows post-war housing at William Barefoot Drive, Coldharbour, in 1955. Note the bin by the lamp standard for the deposit of food scraps to feed pigs, and the elm trees which stood on the field boundaries of Coldharbour Farm.

99 Woolwich Borough Council built the Pippenhall Estate between Southend Crescent and Bexley Road in 1959. The foundations of Barn House, shown being demolished in this picture, now lie under the grass verge between the new flats and Bexley Road. Dr. Fergusson's medical practice was relocated from Barn House to a ground-floor surgery alongside the new flats. The nearby Oakways Estate was built *c.*1961 following the demolition of two Victorian houses named Shrublands and Tanglin.

The First World War

| Lieut. Reeves, Headquarters Staff. | Captain Baker, Headquarters Staff. | Major-General Sir Desmond O'Callaghan, K.C.V.O., Headquarters Staff. | Major Sir Harry North, Commandant 1st Batt., W.K.V.F. | Captain Vansittart, Sidcup. | Lieut. Farnfield, O.C. Sidcup Co., W.K.V.F. | Captain Edmonds, Adjutant 1st Batt., W.K.V.F. | Lieut. Vivian North, King's Royal Rifle Corps. |

100 (*left*) Members of the Eltham Defence Company parade in their non-military attire. This postcard was sent from 28 Greenholm Road on 24 January 1915. The message on the card states that there are 538 members of the Eltham Defence Company due to be inspected by General Sir D. O'Callaghan on the following Saturday—he can be seen on the next picture.

101 (*below left*) These officers are probably associated with the Eltham Defence Company. The picture was taken at Lemonwell, Bexley Road, which was the home of Sir Harry North (son of Colonel North), and his son Vivian North.

102 (*below*) An exercise by the Eltham Defence Company showing two members ready to send a message with semaphore flags.

103 Accommodation for single people engaged on munition work at Woolwich was provided in temporary hostels sited between Well Hall Road and Archery Road. This picture was taken in 1917.

104 This view from Lassa Road shows the hostels in Well Hall Road and a breadcart of J.B. Fyson topped with a Hovis delivery basket.

105 Eltham's newly-built estate for munition workers suffered at the hands of their German counterparts when bombs were dropped from a Zeppelin airship in 1916. The attack occurred during the early hours of 25 August and affected several properties. Total demolition of 210 Well Hall Road can be seen in this picture where three members of the Allen family were killed. They were buried in St John's churchyard. Their home was rebuilt and is now renumbered as 290 Well Hall Road.

106 Zeppelin damage in Dickson Road.

107 A crater in the garden, broken windows, and roof damage to houses in Lovelace Green following the airship raid.

108 Wounded soldiers convalesced at Southwood Hospital using the residential accommodation of Avery Hill College.

109 Southwood Hospital, April 1916.

The Second World War

110 School children and expectant mothers were evacuated from Eltham at the beginning of September 1939. Four evacuees await departure from Pope Street School (now Wyborne School).

111 Most houses had Anderson shelters erected in their gardens. Surface shelters and authorised basements were utilised by members of the public during air raids. This public shelter for 40 people was built at the junction of Bexley Road and Crown Woods Way on part of Avery Hill Farm, and photographed in May 1940.

112 Pope Street School was used by the Auxiliary Fire Service when the children were evacuated. This picture shows unit D4W and their fire appliance in front of a temporary garage.

113 (*above*) These ladies worked for the ambulance service. They were photographed at Archery Road Garage where sandbags have been installed near the petrol pumps.

114 (*right*) Some of the New Eltham wardens photographed in front of a surface shelter at Cambridge Green.

115 (*above*) These shops at Well Hall Road, opposite St John's churchyard, were taken over by Woolwich Borough Council to provide offices for essential services as seen in this picture. The building on the left with the arched entrance previously housed the Eltham Billiard Hall.

116 This Home Guard unit was based in the corner shop to the right of the previous picture. The members were photographed at the rear of the shop in Dobell Road.

117 War damage to the wooden cottage in Crown Woods Way. An older view of the cottage can be seen in picture no.73.

118 This Victory in Europe (VE) party took place in Churchbury Road, Middle Park, on 16 June 1945.

Education

119 A class of girls at Pope Street School, New Eltham, in the 1890s.

120 Five-year-old children at Deansfield School, 1918.

121 The 7th class at Pope Street School in 1921.

122 A class at Eltham Church of England School, Roper Street, 1932.

Babington House School for Girls

NORTH PARK, ELTHAM, S.E.9

The School is situated in 5½ acres of grounds and playing fields. The buildings consist of seven form rooms, two music rooms, laboratory, library, art room, large assembly hall, gymnasium and kindergarten. All classrooms are large and well ventilated. Pupils are prepared for the Oxford School Certificate, London Matriculation, The Societé National des Professeurs de Français en Angleterre, The Royal Drawing Society, The Associated Board of the Royal Academy and Royal College of Music

Illustrated Prospectus sent on application to the Principals :

Miss M. L. Perkins, B.A. Hons. London & Miss A. G. N. Berry, A.R.C.M.

.65

123 Between 1887 and 1959 Babington House School provided a fee-paying education for girls, in premises on the south side of North Park where the flats of Greenacres now stand. A pupil in the mixed kindergarten from 1910 to 1913 was Rex Whistler who later received wide acclaim as an artist. The school moved to Grange Drive, Chislehurst, in 1959. The school advertisement dates from 1935.

124 The Westhorne Senior Boys School Second XI football team 1938-9. The school used premises now known as Briset School.

125 A class at Sidcup Road School in 1950 with their teacher Mr. G. Roberts. This school was established after the Second World War at the Marlborough Sports Club, Sidcup Road, which had been used by the war-time fire service. It was closed in the early 1950s when Greenacres and Ruxley Manor schools were opened in the Coldharbour Estate. The premises were then used, until 1989, as an annexe for Wyborne School. New Eltham Pre-School now operate from this site.

126 Class 4A at Horn Park Junior School. Forty-three children with their teacher, Mr. William Kennett, in 1955. The school opened in 1949 to provide schooling for the many children who had moved into new housing at Horn Park.

Work

127 At the time this picture was taken, in 1904, there were three establishments providing a smith and farrier service in the High Street. One of them, as seen here, was run by Mr. W. Metcalfe at a site where Woolworths now stands. The firm moved to Pound Place in 1905 and continued shoeing horses until 1959. Due to the acquisition of the premises by Sainsbury's, a new shop was opened at Passey Place in 1987 for the sale and repair of lawnmowers.

128 Milk delivery in the 1920s to cottages in Pound Place, which were demolished in 1929 and the site used as a woodyard. The Job Centre opened here in 1981.

129 From 1931 buses terminated at Well Hall Station and parked in Sherard Road. Refreshment facilities were available for the drivers and conductors from this cabin in Station Approach, opposite the station building. This picture was taken in the early 1930s. The cabin survived until 1985 when, together with Well Hall station, it was demolished for construction of the Rochester Way Relief Road (A2).

130 A popular visitor to Rancliffe Gardens was 'Old Joe' who sold ice cream from the side car attached to his motorbike. He would often call just before dinner time on a Sunday as shown in this picture taken in 1936. During the week his pitch was outside the *Royal Mortar* pub at Woolwich New Road.

131 Mr. Walter Grafton established his business at Well Hall in 1913. In 1919 new premises were opened, shown in this picture, at Footscray Road where office machine spools were made. The B&Q store opened in 1988 on the site of the old factory.

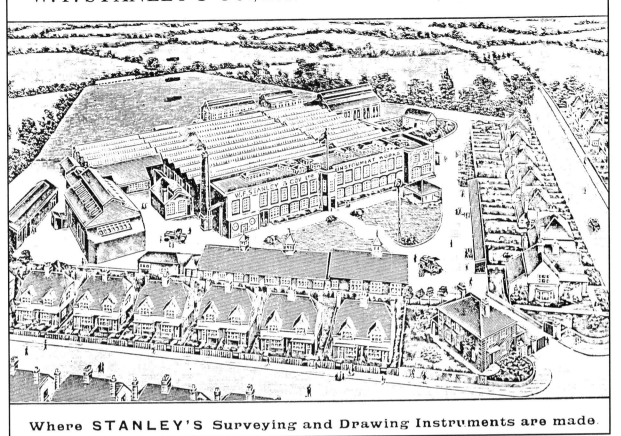

W. F. STANLEY & CO., Ltd. NEW ELTHAM, LONDON, S.E.9.

Where STANLEY'S Surveying and Drawing Instruments are made.

132 The firm of Heath & Co. moved from Crayford to a new factory at New Eltham in 1916 and amalgamated with W.F. Stanley in 1926 and still trade under that name in the production of scientific instruments. The illustration shows the factory set behind the company houses in Lannoy and Avery Hill roads with open space as far as the eye can see!

133 The projectionist at the ABC Cinema, High Street, in April 1972 just prior to its closure.

Leisure

134 The Eltham Band in 1919.

135 Members of the Girls Friendly Society in front of St Luke's Church hall, Westmount Road, in 1925.

136 Bowlers at Well Hall Pleasaunce, *c*.1936. The thatched roof of the pavilion made it unique in Eltham. Since a fire at the pavilion in 1980 the roof has been tiled.

137 The Eltham Dance Studio opened in the late 1930s above Burtons shop at the junction of Well Hall Road and the High Street. After the war the studio was open seven days a week with music by the Eltham Studio Band, who were winners of the 'All Britain 1946' competition.

138 Eltham Cinema was the first purpose-built cinema in Eltham when it opened in 1913. It stood near the junction of the High Street and Westmount Road between the present Mini Town Hall and the Eltham Reservoirs. Some of the operatives are seen here including Maurice Crisp, far left, who was the projectionist for the silent films. The main building was demolished in 1968 having been long out of use as a cinema, though an adjoining rear building survives.

THE
ELTHAM CINEMA
THEATRE, Ltd.,
HIGH STREET, ELTHAM.

Monday, Tuesday & Wednesday, Jan. 26, 27, 28.

THE THIRD XMAS   BRONCHO BILLY RE-
FORMS.   THOSE TROUBLESOME TRESSES.
HIGHLAND ANIMAL STUDIES. Their MUTUAL
FRIEND.   CALINO WATER DIVINER.   THE
TALE OF A HAT. WHAT HAPPENED TO MARY
TOPICAL BUDGET containing ALL THE NEWS.

Thursday, Friday & Saturday, Jan. 29, 30, 31.

PASSING OF JOE MARY.   ALL ON ACCOUNT
OF DAISY.   THE DUMB MESSENGER.
WHERE'S THE BABY? OSCAR'S PREDICAMENT
THE BEAUTIES OF VENICE.   THE GIRL AND
THE GREASER.   IN THE GARDEN FAIR.
TOPICAL BUDGET, containing ALL THE NEWS

FULL TWO HOURS PROGRAMME.
1/-, 6d, and 3d.
Every week day 3 till 5 p.m.; 6 till 10.30 p.m.
Thursday and Saturday 3 till 11 p.m.   (sclm)

139 Programme for the Eltham Cinema, January 1914.

140   The Palace Cinema was built in 1922 by Thomas & Edge of Woolwich for the Kent Cinema Circuit Ltd. There was seating for 1,300 patrons on the ground floor and in the balcony; a tea room, lounge, and smoking room were also provided. The prices of admission were 1s.10d. (balcony), 1s. 3d., and 9d. which included entertainment tax. The dome, decorated with gold leaf, was surmounted by a powerful arc lamp which when lit up could be seen from as far away as Forest Hill and Shooters Hill. The cinema became the ABC in 1963 and was demolished in 1972. Five shops were built on the site at the corner of the High Street and Passey Place.

141 The Odeon Cinema, Well Hall, designed by Andrew Mather, was opened on 20 May 1936 by the Mayor of Woolwich, Councillor Henry Berry, and Sir Ernest Kemp, J.P. The first film shown was *Where's Sally?* In 1973 the premises were converted to a two-screen cinema and in 1981 became the Coronet. Due to its unique architectural style the cinema was designated as a Grade II Listed Building in 1989 by the Department of the Environment.

Souvenir Programme

GRAND OPENING OF THE

ODEON Theatre
REGD.

WELL HALL

MAY 20TH, 1936

142 The Top Rank Bingo Club in 1991. The building opened on 14 April 1938 as the Odeon Cinema, Eltham Hill, with a screening of *Victoria the Great* starring Anna Neagle as the Queen and Anton Walbrook as the Prince Consort. The architect was Andrew Mather who designed a number of cinemas for the Odeon organisation. The cinema was renamed as the Gaumont in 1949 and closed in September 1967. A month later it was officially opened as a bingo hall by comedian Tommy Trinder.

Transport

143 Lewisham station opened in 1849 and the enterprising Mr. Tibbett operated a horse-bus service for Eltham passengers in the days before Eltham was served with a railway.

144 Blackheath station also opened in 1849 and could be reached from Eltham by another horse-bus service. The operator was Thomas Tillings in 1905 when this picture was taken outside the rebuilt *Castle* pub. The last horse bus ran to Blackheath in 1908.

145 (*above*) Victoria Road, now Footscray Road, when traversed by bus route no. 39 between West Kilburn and Sidcup (Black Horse) in 1914.

146 (*right*) The High Street in 1936 with bus 228 picking up passengers outside the Woolwich Borough Council's electricity offices. Until Station Road was lowered by Sidcup station in 1958, the 228 route between Eltham and Chislehurst was restricted to single-decker buses.

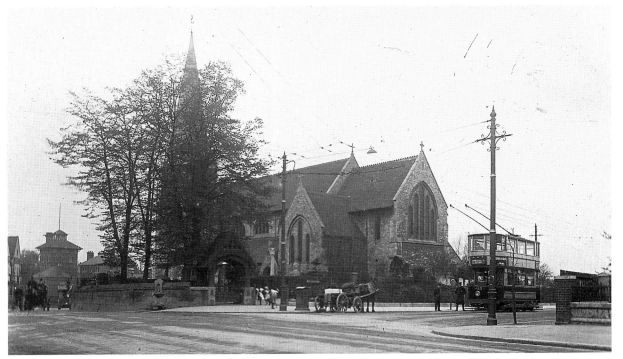

147 (*above*) The terminus of the newly opened Eltham to Woolwich tram route at Well Hall Road, 1910. This route was unique in having the tramcars fitted with a double trolley pole for its overhead power supply, because the scientists at Greenwich Observatory thought that any stray electricity might affect their delicate instruments.

148 The gap in the tram service between Eltham and Lee was completed in two stages. Lee to Lyme Farm, Eltham Hill (by Sherard Road) was opened on 29 November 1920 and the final link to Well Hall Road on 22 March 1921. This picture was taken in the week prior to 5 July 1952 at the High Street by St John's Church when the last trams ran in Eltham, and in London.

149 Well Hall station was opened on 1 May 1895 when the Bexleyheath Line was completed between Blackheath and Dartford. The timber-clad station building can be seen in the centre of the picture, *c*.1906, with trucks in the goods yard located between the station and Well Hall Lane where the workmen are standing. The road is now known as Sherard Road and recently the housing development of Pullman Place has been constructed on the former goods yard.

150 Eltham Park station, on the Bexleyheath line, was known as Shooters Hill station when it opened on 1 July 1908. This picture shows the main office building of the newly-opened station. This building was converted into five shops, known as Station Parade, in 1922 following the relocation of the ticket office at platform level. The former ticket office became a chemist shop. Electric trains were introduced in 1926. The station closed in 1985 but the shops remain.

151 George Dickerson, Haulage Contractor, Karrier Lodge, Avery Hill Road, was the operator of this lorry seen working on the Eltham Heights Estate c.1936. The yard at the junction of Avery Hill and Cradley roads was bought by Mr Dickerson in 1932 and is still in operation as a family business in 1995.

Shops and Services

152 Court Yard, 1902. The shops from the left are: W. James, greengrocer, S. Harler, bootmaker and leather seller (two shops), O. Barratt, tobacconist, C. Mitchell, watchmaker, O. Barratt, hairdresser, *The Crown Inn*, F. Millington landlord. Between the pub and the terrace of cottages was Crown Alley. The old tree shown here was blown down by a strong wind in 1903. The block of three shops next to *The Crown* was built in 1810 and survives today.

153 Mellins, the Eltham Pharmacy, mid-1920s. The business was established by Charles Mellin in the 1860s and he managed the firm for nearly forty years. The pictures shows Mr. H. Steward, the pharmacist, outside the shop which may be decorated for the 1926 Eltham Shopping Week. Mr. Steward died in 1928. Since 1976 the premises has been used as a restaurant trading as Mellins.

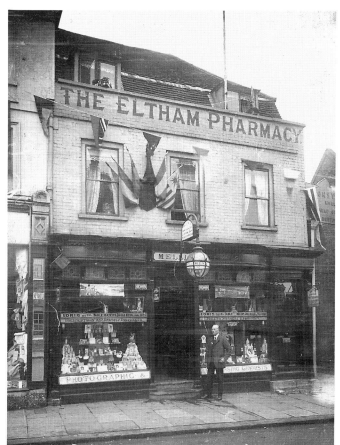

154 The British Bakery (J.B. Fyson), 94 High Street, 1916. This bakery stood between Cave Austin's grocery shop to the left and the cobbled yard that led to Elizabeth Terrace. The yard can be seen today between Boots and W.H. Smith.

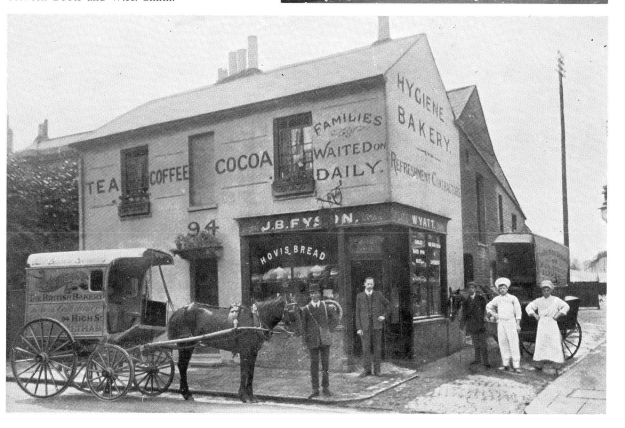

155 The Co-operative Pharmacy in the High Street opened on 4 December 1935 in premises that, since 1920, had been used by the Co-op as a food shop. In 1994 Co-op Travel took over this shop when the pharmacy moved to Court Yard.

156 The Home and Colonial Stores, High Street, *c.*1914. The notice in the window refers to a 'Tea Crisis'. Clarks Bakery now operate from this shop.

157 High Street, *c.*1904. The shop of Watkins, gas engineer, to the right is at the corner of Roper Street. Allders store now stands where A.J. Glock once traded, and the garden to the left is that of Ivy House which is now the site of the Co-op. Notice the width of the road.

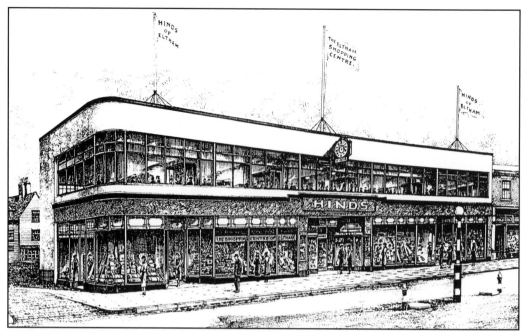

158 Hinds store was opened on 10 February 1934 by Mr. C.P. Hinds, chairman of the parent company at Blackheath. The picture, by Llwyd Roberts, shows the newly built store.

159 Alterations to Hinds were made in 1936 which included extra floors, a lift (still in operation), and a roof garden. The store now trades as Allders.

160 Eltham House, High Street, 1937. This Georgian house was taken over by the South Metropolitan Gas Company in 1916 and included an orangery at the end of the rear garden. The house was demolished in 1937 to make way for a new gas showroom and Marks and Spencer. The Orangery, as can be seen in picture no.31, survives—almost.

161 Marks and Spencer, 1963. The store opened on 11 February 1938 and specialised in clothing. Trading ceased at the end of November 1975 when the business was transferred to new premises built on the site of the former British Road Services depot.

162 The Broadway, High Street, probably at the time of the Coronation of King George V in 1911. These shops can still be seen today but the rest of the scene has changed. The structure with the spire was known as 'The Monument' but was no more than a fumigation shaft over a sewer. Further along Bexley Road is Conduit Lodge and Barn House.

163 The Parade, Footscray Road, New Eltham, *c.*1932. The nine shops going from right to left are: Express Dairy, Bridgland & Curtis, grocers, S.F. Henly, newsagent, F.J. Langford, baker, H. Collett as Bartlett's Stores (two shops), draper, New Eltham Fisheries, F. Grove, butcher, T.J. Robins, grocer.

164 The first Co-op shop at New Eltham was officially opened on 20 July 1921 and drew an enthusiastic crowd. This temporary structure, sited next to the New Eltham station master's house on the left, was replaced by the present store in 1931.

165 High Road, Mottingham, *c*.1912. The grocery shop, and post office, of W.J. Brisley is at the junction with Portland Road. Beyond W.J. Brisley there were six houses and five shops which included a chemist at the corner of Clarence Road. All these buildings were destroyed by enemy action in the Second World War and replaced by flats.

166 The Well Hall Stores of C. Barrett, Well Hall Road at the junction with Dunvegan Road, 1903. The shop continued as an ironmongers for many years but since 1991 has been divided into two shops.

167 The Royal Arsenal Co-operative Society opened a new store at Well Hall on 25 June 1906 with the help of 36 decorated horse-drawn vehicles and the band of the Royal West Kent Regiment. This picture was taken in the 1950s; from November 1964 a new Co-op store was operating on this site.

Public Services

168 Eltham Cottage Hospital, High Street, was established in 1880 at this building near St John's Church. A new hospital was built in 1898 at Park Place (now Passey Place) and remains in use as Eltham and Mottingham House. The original hospital building was bought by Mr. W. Hitches and incorporated into his new cycle and motor business. Beadles now sell cars from this site.

169 The post office, Park Place, *c*.1915 was opened on 12 June 1912 and replaced a smaller office in Court Yard. The Park Place frontage was doubled in size in 1935 and a sorting office and garage were built at the rear. The post office returned to Court Yard in 1972 where it operates today. The former post office building at Passey Place was opened as *The Old Post Office* public house on 23 May 1995, by Regent Inns.

e Station, High Street, Eltham,

K. G. Digby,
Eltham.

170 Eltham fire station was opened on 8 December 1904 by Edward Smith, Chairman of the London County Council Fire Brigade Committee, who had earlier laid the foundation stone on 27 February. The first appliances were horse-drawn. This picture is probably *c.*1916. The fire station lost its frontage in 1933 for the widening of the High Street.

171 Between 1865 and 1939 this building, at the junction of the High Street and Victoria Road (Footscray Road), was Eltham police station. While being driven to his new estate at Broome, near Canterbury, in 1914, Lord Kitchener, whose face appeared on recruiting posters for the First World War, was involved in an accident with another car at this road junction. Lord Kitchener survived this mishap and was taken into the police station to await another car.

172 Eltham Health Centre, at the corner of Westhorne Avenue and Briset Road, was opened by the Minister of Health, the Rt. Hon. Arthur Greenwood, on 14 February 1931. Demolished by enemy action in March 1941, it was not rebuilt.

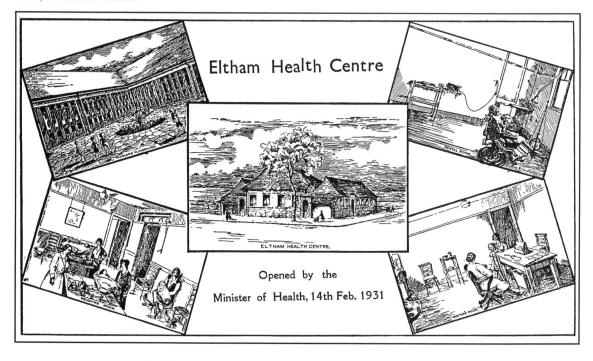

Events

173 Elizabeth Terrace. The message on the back of this postcard records that, 'This is considered the best and prettiest part of Eltham's decorations for Coronation Day (King George V)'. 11 July 1911. The Kingdom Hall of Jehovah's Witnesses now stands on the site of the four cottages on the left of the picture.

WEST WOOLWICH PARLIAMENTARY ELECTION

GEORGE WANSBROUGH

LABOUR CANDIDATE

will address the following

ELTHAM MEETINGS

THURSDAY NEXT, NOV. 7th, at 8 p.m.

CO-OPERATIVE HALL
FOOTSCRAY ROAD

SUPPORTED BY :—

LORD STRABOLGI

MONDAY, NOVEMBER 11th, at 8 p.m.

CATHOLIC HALL
APPLETON ROAD

TUESDAY, NOVEMBER 12th, at 8 p.m.

KING'S PARK L.C.C. SCHOOL
ELTHAM PALACE ROAD

WEDNESDAY, NOVEMBER 13th, at 8 p.m.

PROGRESS HALL
ADMIRAL SEYMOUR ROAD

A hearty invitation to attend is given to all electors.

WEST WOOLWICH PARLIAMENTARY ELECTION, 1935
Polling Day: Thursday, November 14th

VOTE FOR
SIR KINGSLEY
WOOD

PEACE — SECURITY — PROGRESS

EVENING MEETINGS

FOX HILL SCHOOLS	....	TUES.	5th Nov.	8 p.m.
HAIMO ROAD SCHOOLS	....	WED.	6th Nov.	8 p.m.
POPE STREET SCHOOLS	....	THURS.	7th Nov.	8 p.m.
EGLINTON ROAD SCHOOLS	...	THURS.	7th Nov.	8 p.m.
GORDON SCHOOLS, ELTHAM	....	FRI.	8th Nov.	8 p.m.
WOOD STREET SCHOOLS	....	TUES.	12th Nov.	8 p.m.

EVE OF THE POLL RALLY

PARISH HALL, ELTHAM	....	WED.	13th Nov.	8 p.m.
St. PETER'S HALL, LEE	....	WED.	13th Nov.	8 p.m.

WOMEN'S MEETINGS

BRIDGEMAN HALL, SOUTHWOOD RD. NEW ELTHAM	TUES.	5th Nov.	3 p.m.
PLUMSTEAD COMMON CONSERVATIVE CLUB HALL, PLUMSTEAD COMMON ROAD	TUES.	5th Nov.	3 p.m.
PARISH HALL, ELTHAM	WED.	6th Nov.	3 p.m.
KINGSLEY HALL, THOMAS STREET WOOLWICH	WED.	6th Nov.	3 p.m.
St. LUKE'S HALL, WESTMOUNT ROAD, ELTHAM	THURS.	7th Nov.	3 p.m.

(1)

WEST WOOLWICH RESULT.

The counting of the votes in West Woolwich took place at Woolwich Town Hall last night under the direction of Mr. David Jenkins, Acting Returning Officer.

The result was as follows:—

Wood, Sir Kingsley (Cons.) 24,649

Wansbrough, G. (Lab.) ... 17,373

Majority 7,276

No Change.

1931 ELECTION.

WOOD, Sir Kingsley (Con.) 26,441

REEVES, J. (Lab.) 14,520

Conservative majority 11,921

---

174 General Election, 1935, meetings and result.

```
Eltham's Members of Parliament
------------------------------
From 1832 to 1885 Eltham was part of the Western Division of
Kent. From 1885 to 1918 it was part of Woolwich. Due to an
expanding population Woolwich was split into two constituencies
and Eltham became part of West Woolwich from 1918 to 1983. The
name 'Eltham' was given to the constituency in 1983.


MPs for Woolwich West
---------------------
  Sir H.Kingsley Wood      (Con.)    1918-43
  Major Francis Beech      (Con.)    1943-5
  Henry Berry              (Lab.)    1945-50
  Sir William Steward      (Con.)    1950-9
  Colin Turner             (Con.)    1959-64
  William Hamling          (Lab.)    1964-75
  Peter Bottomley          (Con.)    1975-83


MP for Eltham since 1983
Peter Bottomley
```

175   Eltham's Members of Parliament. From 1832 to 1885 Eltham was part of the Western Division of Kent. From 1885 to 1918 it was part of Woolwich. Due to an expanding population Woolwich was split into two constituencies and Eltham became part of West Woolwich from 1918 to 1983. The name 'Eltham' was given to the constituency in 1983.

176   The Rt. Hon. John Burns, P.C. opened the Tudor Barn and Art Gallery at Well Hall Pleasaunce on 23 May 1936. He is seen here opening the door, standing next to the Mayor of Woolwich, Councillor Henry Berry, and the Town Clerk, David Jenkins.

177 Frankie Howerd returned to St Barnabas Church, Rochester Way, on 23 October 1988 for the renaming of the church hall as The Frankie Howerd Community Centre. The comedian lived in Eltham from the age of two and had many happy associations with the church. The picture shows Frankie Howerd pouring a drink for Peter Bottomley, M.P., while Mayor of Greenwich, Councillor John Austin Walker, waits for his tipple.

178 Bob Hope visited the Bob Hope Theatre, Wythfield Road, on 27 August 1991 to unveil a plaque commemorating the opening of an extension to the building. Bob Hope was born at 44 Craigton Road, Eltham, on 29 May 1903 and has given financial support to the theatre which he visited in 1980 and 1982.

179 The Eltham Town Sign was unveiled at Passey Place on 11 September 1993 by Marion Kennett, Chairman of The Eltham Society, sponsors of the scheme. The sign, designed by Paul Cookson, features St John's Church, Avery Hill Winter Gardens, Eltham Palace and bridge, Tudor Barn and Severndroog Castle.

Advertisements of September 1901 and November 1907 from Holy Trinity church magazine